From Words to Worlds Exploring Multilingual Education through Student-Centered Curriculum Design

Amalie

TABLE OF CONTENTS

Chapter 1: Introduction to Multilingual Education

Understanding Multilingualism

In today's globalized world, multilingualism has become increasingly important. The ability to speak multiple languages not only enhances communication skills but also opens up a world of opportunities, both academically and professionally. This subchapter aims to provide students with a comprehensive understanding of multilingualism and its significance in the field of curriculum development and instructional design.

Multilingualism refers to the ability to communicate in two or more languages proficiently. It is not limited to individuals who have acquired languages from birth but also includes those who have learned additional languages through formal education or immersion programs. Multilingualism is a valuable asset in the current educational landscape as it promotes cultural diversity, global understanding, and cognitive development.

From the perspective of curriculum development and instructional design, understanding multilingualism is crucial for creating inclusive and effective learning environments. By acknowledging and embracing students' linguistic diversity, curriculum designers can develop student-centered approaches that cater to their unique linguistic backgrounds and promote equitable access to education.

One key aspect of understanding multilingualism is recognizing the different types of multilingualism. These include simultaneous multilingualism, where individuals acquire multiple languages from birth, and sequential multilingualism, where individuals learn additional languages later in life. By understanding the different multilingual profiles of students, curriculum designers can tailor instruction to meet their specific needs and provide appropriate language support.

Moreover, understanding the benefits of multilingualism can motivate students to embrace language learning. Multilingualism has been linked to enhanced cognitive abilities, such as improved problem-solving skills, creativity, and flexibility in thinking. It also fosters cross-cultural understanding, promotes empathy, and enables individuals to engage with diverse communities on a global scale.

Incorporating multilingualism in curriculum development and instructional design also requires a focus on language policies and practices. Students should be aware of the importance of maintaining and promoting their languages, as well as the benefits of being able to communicate in multiple languages. Curriculum designers can support this by incorporating multilingual resources, encouraging code-switching, and providing opportunities for students to showcase their linguistic abilities.

In conclusion, understanding multilingualism is essential for students pursuing careers in curriculum development and instructional design. By recognizing the importance of multilingualism, students can create inclusive and effective learning environments that value linguistic diversity and promote equitable access to education. Embracing multilingualism not only enriches students' educational experiences but also prepares them for a globalized and interconnected world.

Importance of Multilingual Education

The Importance of Multilingual Education

In today's globalized world, the ability to communicate in multiple languages is becoming increasingly important. Multilingual education offers students a wide range of benefits, both academically and personally. This subchapter explores the significance of multilingual education and its role in student-centered curriculum design.

First and foremost, multilingual education enhances cognitive abilities. Research has shown that learning multiple languages stimulates brain development, improves memory, and enhances problem-solving skills. By engaging in multilingual education, students are exposed to different linguistic structures and patterns, enabling them to think more flexibly and creatively. This cognitive flexibility is essential in today's rapidly changing job market, where individuals with diverse language skills are highly sought after.

Furthermore, multilingual education promotes cultural understanding and acceptance. By learning different languages, students gain a deeper insight into various cultures, traditions, and ways of life. This exposure fosters empathy and respect towards different ethnicities and backgrounds, creating a more inclusive and harmonious society. In an increasingly interconnected world, the ability to communicate with people from diverse cultural backgrounds is crucial for social cohesion and global cooperation.

Moreover, multilingual education opens up a plethora of opportunities for personal and professional growth. In an era of globalization, businesses are expanding their operations across borders, creating a demand for individuals who can communicate with international clients and colleagues. By acquiring proficiency in multiple languages, students increase their employability and open doors to a broader range of career paths. Additionally, multilingualism provides individuals with the freedom to travel, explore new cultures, and build meaningful connections with people from different parts of the world.

In the context of student-centered curriculum design, multilingual education promotes a more inclusive and equitable learning environment. By incorporating diverse languages into the curriculum, educators ensure that all students, regardless of their linguistic background, have equal opportunities to thrive academically. This approach recognizes and values the linguistic diversity within the student population, fostering a sense of belonging and encouraging students to embrace their unique linguistic identities.

In conclusion, multilingual education is of utmost importance in today's interconnected world. It enhances cognitive abilities, promotes cultural understanding, opens up opportunities for personal and professional growth, and fosters inclusivity in student-centered curriculum design. By embracing multilingual education, students can equip themselves with the skills necessary to navigate a globalized society and become responsible global citizens.

Challenges in Multilingual Education

In the ever-evolving landscape of education, multilingualism has emerged as a key focus area. As the world becomes more globalized, the demand for multilingual individuals who can effectively communicate and interact across cultures is on the rise. Multilingual education plays a crucial role in equipping students with the necessary skills to thrive in this interconnected world. However, it is not without its challenges.

One of the primary challenges in multilingual education is the design of a student-centered curriculum that caters to the diverse linguistic backgrounds of learners. Curriculum development and instructional design specialists face the task of creating a curriculum that is inclusive, engaging, and effective for students from various linguistic backgrounds. This requires a deep understanding of the linguistic and cultural diversity within the student population.

Another challenge is the availability of resources and materials in multiple languages. It is essential to provide students with a wide range of resources that reflect their linguistic backgrounds and experiences. However, finding appropriate resources that match the curriculum objectives can be a daunting task. Curriculum developers and instructional designers need to tap into a variety of sources, such as literature, digital platforms, and community resources, to ensure that students have access to materials that support their language development.

Assessment and evaluation pose yet another challenge in multilingual education. Traditional assessment methods may not accurately measure the linguistic and cognitive abilities of multilingual students. Curriculum developers and instructional designers must explore alternative assessment strategies that take into account the diverse language proficiencies and cultural perspectives of learners. This requires a shift towards more authentic and performance-based assessments that capture a broader range of language skills and knowledge.

Furthermore, the implementation of multilingual education can face resistance from various stakeholders. Some may question the value of teaching multiple languages or express concerns about the potential dilution of the dominant language. Curriculum developers and instructional designers need to address these concerns by emphasizing the cognitive, social, and cultural benefits of multilingualism. They should also foster collaboration and communication between all stakeholders to build a shared understanding and commitment towards multilingual education.

In conclusion, multilingual education presents both opportunities and challenges for curriculum development and instructional design specialists. By addressing the challenges of designing a student-centered curriculum, providing appropriate resources, developing alternative assessment strategies, and fostering collaboration, educators can create an inclusive and effective multilingual education system. Through their efforts, students can develop the necessary language skills and intercultural competence to thrive in an increasingly interconnected world.

Chapter 2: Foundations of Curriculum Design

Theoretical Frameworks for Curriculum Design

As students pursuing a career in curriculum development and instructional design, it is crucial to understand the various theoretical frameworks that guide curriculum design. These frameworks provide a solid foundation for creating effective and student-centered educational programs. In this subchapter, we will explore some of the most prominent theoretical frameworks for curriculum design.

One widely recognized framework is the Constructivist approach, which emphasizes active learning and student engagement. According to this perspective, students construct their knowledge through hands-on activities, problem-solving, and collaboration. The curriculum design under this framework focuses on creating real-world connections, promoting critical thinking skills, and encouraging students to become active participants in their own learning.

Another important framework is the Behaviorist approach, which views learning as a process of acquiring new behaviors through reinforcement and repetition. In this framework, curriculum design revolves around clearly defined objectives, systematic instruction, and frequent assessments to measure learning outcomes. This approach often includes explicit instruction, drill and practice activities, and behavior management strategies.

A humanistic framework emphasizes the holistic development of students, considering their emotional, social, and cognitive needs. The curriculum design guided by this framework aims to foster personal growth, self-esteem, and self-actualization. It often includes student-centered activities, cooperative learning, and opportunities for self-reflection.

The Sociocultural framework recognizes the influence of social and cultural factors on learning. This framework emphasizes the importance of collaboration, cultural responsiveness, and the integration of students' backgrounds and experiences into the curriculum. It promotes the development of critical consciousness and encourages students to become agents of change in their communities.

Lastly, the Cognitive framework focuses on understanding how students process and organize information. It emphasizes the development of thinking skills, problem-solving abilities, and metacognition. The curriculum design guided by this framework often includes inquiry-based learning, concept mapping, and the use of technology to enhance cognitive processes.

By familiarizing ourselves with these theoretical frameworks, we can approach curriculum design with a solid theoretical foundation. This knowledge enables us to create educational programs that are engaging, effective, and tailored to the needs of diverse learners. As future curriculum developers and instructional designers, it is essential to continually explore and adapt these frameworks to meet the evolving demands of education.

Student-Centered Approach

In today's rapidly changing world, education plays a pivotal role in preparing students for success in their personal and professional lives. Traditional methods of teaching focused on a one-size-fits-all approach, where students were passive recipients of knowledge. However, educational research has shown that a student-centered approach is more effective in engaging students, fostering their creativity, and ensuring their long-term retention of knowledge.

A student-centered approach puts the learner at the forefront of the educational process. It recognizes that each student is unique, with different strengths, learning styles, and interests. By tailoring instruction to individual students, educators can create a more engaging and meaningful learning experience.

One key aspect of the student-centered approach is curriculum design. Curriculum development and instructional design professionals are at the forefront of creating educational materials that are centered around the needs and interests of students. They understand the importance of incorporating student input, allowing them to take ownership of their learning, and fostering their autonomy.

In this subchapter, we will delve into the concept of the student-centered approach, exploring its principles and benefits. We will discuss how curriculum development and instructional design professionals can contribute to creating student-centered learning experiences.

One principle of the student-centered approach is the recognition of the importance of active learning. Instead of passively receiving information, students are encouraged to actively participate in their learning process. This can be achieved through various strategies such as group work, project-based learning, and problem-solving activities.

Another key aspect of the student-centered approach is the promotion of critical thinking skills. Students are encouraged to analyze, evaluate, and synthesize information, enabling them to become independent and lifelong learners. This approach fosters creativity, innovation, and problem-solving abilities that are essential for success in the 21st century.

Furthermore, the student-centered approach emphasizes the importance of meaningful and authentic assessments. Assessments are designed to measure students' understanding and application of knowledge, rather than mere memorization of facts. This allows educators to gain valuable insights into students' progress and tailor instruction accordingly.

In conclusion, the student-centered approach is a transformative paradigm in education. It empowers students to become active participants in their learning journey, fostering their creativity, critical thinking skills, and autonomy. Curriculum development and instructional design professionals play a vital role in implementing this approach by creating engaging and meaningful learning experiences. By embracing the student-centered approach, students can develop the skills and knowledge they need to thrive in our ever-evolving world.

Multilingual Pedagogy

Multilingual Pedagogy: Unlocking the World of Multilingual Education

In today's increasingly interconnected world, the ability to communicate in multiple languages has become a valuable asset. With globalization and multiculturalism on the rise, multilingualism is no longer a luxury but a necessity. As students, you have a unique opportunity to embrace and harness the power of multilingualism through an innovative approach called multilingual pedagogy.

Multilingual pedagogy is a student-centered curriculum design that celebrates linguistic diversity and promotes the development of multiple languages. It recognizes the inherent value of students' home languages and seeks to integrate them into the educational experience. By doing so, it not only enhances students' linguistic skills but also fosters a sense of identity, cultural pride, and inclusivity.

One of the key principles of multilingual pedagogy is the recognition that every student is a language learner. This approach acknowledges that students bring a wealth of linguistic knowledge and experiences to the classroom, regardless of their proficiency levels. By embracing students' diverse linguistic backgrounds, multilingual pedagogy creates an inclusive learning environment where each student's unique linguistic talents are nurtured and celebrated.

Furthermore, multilingual pedagogy encourages the use of students' home languages as a resource for learning. Rather than dismissing or devaluing students' native languages, it leverages them to enhance the acquisition of other languages. This approach promotes translanguaging, a process where students use their entire linguistic repertoire to make meaning and understand concepts. By allowing students to draw on their existing language skills, multilingual pedagogy provides a solid foundation for language development and facilitates a deeper understanding of content across various subjects.

In addition to its linguistic benefits, multilingual pedagogy also contributes to the development of critical thinking skills, empathy, and intercultural competence. By engaging with different languages and cultures, students gain a broader perspective of the world and learn to appreciate and respect diversity. They become more equipped to navigate a globalized society and communicate effectively in various contexts.

As students interested in curriculum development and instructional design, embracing multilingual pedagogy opens up a world of possibilities. By incorporating this approach into your future educational endeavors, you can create inclusive and culturally responsive learning environments that empower students to become confident, skilled, and compassionate global citizens.

In conclusion, multilingual pedagogy is a transformative approach that recognizes and celebrates linguistic diversity in education. By valuing students' home languages, promoting translanguaging, and fostering intercultural understanding, this pedagogy equips students with the necessary skills to thrive in a multilingual and interconnected world. Embrace multilingual pedagogy, and unlock the door to a world of endless opportunities.

Chapter 3: Multilingual Curriculum Development

Needs Assessment and Analysis

In the world of curriculum development and instructional design, one of the essential steps to ensure effective education is conducting a thorough needs assessment and analysis. This process allows educators to understand the specific requirements, challenges, and strengths of the students they serve, ultimately leading to the creation of student-centered curriculum design.

A needs assessment involves gathering relevant data and information about the learners, their cultural background, language proficiency, academic abilities, and individual needs. This data is then analyzed to identify the gaps between the students' current knowledge and skills and the desired learning outcomes. By understanding these gaps, educators can tailor the curriculum and instructional strategies to meet the unique needs of each student.

The first step in conducting a needs assessment is to gather data through various methods such as surveys, interviews, observations, and standardized tests. These methods provide valuable insights into the students' learning preferences, interests, and strengths. Additionally, it is crucial to involve all stakeholders, including students, parents, teachers, and community members, in the needs assessment process. Their input and perspectives are invaluable in gaining a comprehensive understanding of the students' needs.

Once the data is collected, it is time to analyze and interpret the findings. This analysis helps identify patterns, trends, and areas of improvement. Educators can identify common challenges faced by students, such as language barriers, lack of resources, or cultural differences. They can also identify areas where students excel, allowing for the incorporation of these strengths into the curriculum design.

Based on the needs assessment and analysis, educators can develop specific learning objectives and outcomes that align with the students' needs and aspirations. The curriculum can then be designed to address these objectives, incorporating appropriate teaching strategies, materials, and assessments. By ensuring that the curriculum is student-centered, educators can create an inclusive and engaging learning environment that promotes active participation and meaningful learning experiences.

In conclusion, needs assessment and analysis are indispensable steps in curriculum development and instructional design. By understanding the unique needs of the students, educators can create student-centered curricula that cater to diverse learners. By involving all stakeholders and utilizing various data collection methods, educators can gather comprehensive and accurate information about the students' needs. This information, when analyzed and interpreted, allows educators to identify areas of improvement and develop tailored learning objectives. Ultimately, a well-designed curriculum that addresses the needs of the students fosters effective education and enriches the learning experiences of all students.

Setting Learning Objectives

Setting clear and measurable learning objectives is a crucial step in curriculum development and instructional design. Learning objectives serve as a roadmap that guides students in their educational journey, helping them to understand what is expected of them and what they will be able to achieve by the end of a course or program. In this subchapter, we will explore the importance of setting learning objectives and provide practical tips on how to create effective and meaningful objectives.

Why are learning objectives important? Learning objectives provide a clear sense of direction for both students and educators. They help students to understand what they will be able to do or know after completing a specific module or course. Learning objectives also enable educators to design appropriate instructional strategies and assessment methods that align with the desired outcomes. By setting clear objectives, students can better focus their efforts, monitor their progress, and stay motivated throughout their learning journey.

When setting learning objectives, it is important to ensure they are specific, measurable, achievable, relevant, and time-bound (SMART). Specific objectives clearly define what students should be able to do or know. Measurable objectives provide a clear way to assess whether the learning outcome has been achieved. Achievable objectives are realistic and attainable within the given context and resources. Relevant objectives are aligned with the overall goals and curriculum of the course or program. Time-bound objectives specify when the learning outcome should be achieved.

To create effective and meaningful learning objectives, start by understanding the desired learning outcomes of the course or program. Consider the knowledge, skills, and attitudes that students should acquire. Break down the desired outcomes into smaller, manageable objectives that are aligned with the course content and assessments. Use action verbs such as "analyze," "compare," "synthesize," or "evaluate" to clearly articulate the expected behaviors or cognitive processes.

Furthermore, engage students in the process of setting learning objectives. By involving them, you empower students to take ownership of their learning and make the objectives more relevant and meaningful to their individual goals. Encourage students to reflect on their own learning needs and to set personal objectives that align with the broader course objectives. This process not only enhances student motivation but also fosters a sense of responsibility and self-direction.

In conclusion, setting clear and measurable learning objectives is essential for effective curriculum development and instructional design. Learning objectives provide a roadmap for students, enabling them to understand what is expected and what they will achieve. By following the SMART guidelines and involving students in the process, educators can create meaningful and relevant objectives that enhance student motivation and facilitate successful learning outcomes.

Designing Multilingual Units and Lessons

As students studying curriculum development and instructional design, it is crucial to understand the importance of designing multilingual units and lessons in today's diverse educational settings. In a world that is becoming increasingly interconnected and globalized, multilingual education plays a vital role in fostering inclusivity, promoting cultural understanding, and enhancing academic success for all students.

The concept of multilingual education goes beyond simply teaching multiple languages; it involves incorporating diverse linguistic and cultural backgrounds into the curriculum design process. By acknowledging and valuing the linguistic resources that students bring to the classroom, educators can create a student-centered learning environment that celebrates diversity and promotes language development for all learners.

When designing multilingual units and lessons, it is essential to consider the following key principles:

1. Culturally Responsive Pedagogy: Designing units and lessons that reflect the cultural backgrounds and experiences of students helps create a sense of belonging and engagement. Incorporating authentic materials, literature, and examples from diverse cultures allows students to see themselves represented in the curriculum.

2. Language Integration: Integrating multiple languages throughout the curriculum helps students develop both their first language and the language of instruction. This approach recognizes the value of students' home languages and supports their academic progress in the language of instruction.

3. Differentiated Instruction: Recognizing the diverse language proficiency levels and learning needs of students is crucial. Designing units and lessons that provide different entry points and scaffolding strategies allows for the inclusion of all learners, regardless of their language background.

4. Collaborative Learning: Encouraging collaboration and interaction among students from different linguistic backgrounds fosters peer-to-peer learning, promotes language development, and enhances intercultural competence.

5. Assessment and Feedback: Designing appropriate assessment tools that value students' multilingual abilities is essential. Providing constructive feedback that acknowledges students' linguistic growth and encourages further development supports their language acquisition journey.

By incorporating these principles into the design of multilingual units and lessons, students can experience a curriculum that is inclusive, culturally responsive, and promotes linguistic development. As future curriculum developers and instructional designers, it is our responsibility to advocate for and implement multilingual education practices that empower all students, regardless of their linguistic background, to thrive in today's interconnected world.

In conclusion, designing multilingual units and lessons is a crucial aspect of curriculum development and instructional design. By embracing the principles of culturally responsive pedagogy, language integration, differentiated instruction, collaborative learning, and appropriate assessment, we can create a curriculum that celebrates diversity, promotes language development, and fosters academic success for all students. Let us embrace the power of multilingual education and create inclusive and empowering learning environments for students across the globe.

Chapter 4: Instructional Design Strategies

Differentiated Instruction

Differentiated Instruction: Nurturing Individual Learning Paths

In the ever-evolving landscape of education, the concept of differentiated instruction has gained significant recognition and prominence. As students, it is crucial to understand its significance and how it can positively impact our educational journey. This subchapter aims to shed light on differentiated instruction and its role in empowering students through student-centered curriculum design, as outlined in the book "From Words to Worlds: Exploring Multilingual Education through Student-Centered Curriculum Design."

Differentiated instruction is an approach that acknowledges the unique needs, abilities, and interests of each student. It encourages educators to tailor their teaching methods, content, and assessments to cater to individual students' diverse learning styles and preferences. This approach recognizes the fact that no two students are alike and that a one-size-fits-all model of education falls short in addressing the needs of all learners.

By embracing differentiated instruction, curriculum development and instructional design can be transformed into a dynamic and inclusive process. It seeks to create a learning environment that promotes active engagement, collaboration, and critical thinking. Through this approach, students are empowered to take ownership of their learning, fostering a sense of autonomy and self-efficacy.

One of the key benefits of differentiated instruction is its ability to meet students where they are academically and emotionally. It ensures that every student receives the necessary support and challenge to maximize their potential. This tailored approach not only optimizes learning outcomes but also enhances students' overall motivation and engagement.

Moreover, differentiated instruction promotes cultural and linguistic diversity by valuing students' unique backgrounds and experiences. It recognizes the importance of multilingual education and the benefits it brings to students in an increasingly interconnected world. By incorporating students' native languages and cultural perspectives into the curriculum, differentiated instruction fosters a sense of belonging and inclusivity.

To effectively implement differentiated instruction, collaboration between students, teachers, and parents is crucial. Open lines of communication and ongoing feedback enable educators to continuously adapt and refine their instructional practices. Additionally, students play an active role in setting goals, reflecting on their progress, and advocating for their individual needs.

In conclusion, differentiated instruction is a powerful approach that transforms curriculum development and instructional design into a student-centered process. By embracing students' unique needs, abilities, and interests, this approach nurtures individual learning paths and fosters a diverse and inclusive educational environment. As students, we have the opportunity to advocate for differentiated instruction, ensuring that our educational journey is tailored to our individual strengths and aspirations.

Project-Based Learning

In the realm of education, there is a growing emphasis on student-centered curriculum design, which places the learner at the heart of the educational process. One approach that aligns perfectly with this philosophy is project-based learning (PBL). This subchapter aims to introduce students to the concept of project-based learning, its benefits, and how it can be effectively implemented in their educational journey.

Project-based learning is an instructional approach that encourages students to actively engage in real-world problems or challenges. It goes beyond traditional classroom teaching by providing students with opportunities to apply their knowledge and skills in practical and meaningful ways. By working on projects, students not only deepen their understanding of the subject matter but also develop essential skills such as critical thinking, problem-solving, collaboration, and communication.

The benefits of project-based learning are numerous. Firstly, it promotes student motivation and engagement. By working on projects that are relevant and interesting to them, students become more invested in their learning. They develop a sense of ownership and pride in their work, which in turn leads to increased self-confidence and a desire for further exploration.

Secondly, project-based learning fosters creativity and innovation. Students are encouraged to think outside the box, find unique solutions to problems, and showcase their individual talents. This approach nurtures a growth mindset, where mistakes are seen as opportunities for learning and improvement.

Furthermore, project-based learning supports the development of essential 21st-century skills. In today's rapidly changing world, it is crucial for students to be adaptable, collaborative, and effective communicators. Through project-based learning, students learn how to work in teams, effectively communicate their ideas, and adapt to different situations – skills that will serve them well in their future careers.

To implement project-based learning effectively, students need to follow a structured process. This involves identifying a project topic, setting goals, conducting research, planning and organizing their work, implementing their ideas, and finally, reflecting on their learning. By following these steps, students can ensure that their projects are well-executed and meet their intended objectives.

In conclusion, project-based learning offers students an exciting and engaging approach to education. By immersing themselves in real-world challenges and working collaboratively, students not only deepen their understanding of the subject matter but also develop essential skills for success in the 21st century. As students, embracing project-based learning can empower you to take control of your education, explore your passions, and make a real impact on the world around you. So, let your curiosity guide you, and embark on a journey of learning through projects!

Technology Integration in Multilingual Education

In today's interconnected world, the need for multilingual education has become increasingly important. As societies become more diverse and globalized, it is crucial for students to develop proficiency in multiple languages. However, implementing effective multilingual education programs can be a complex task. This is where technology integration plays a vital role.

Technology has revolutionized the way we teach and learn, and its integration in multilingual education has the potential to enhance students' language acquisition and overall educational experience. In this subchapter, we will explore the various ways technology can be integrated into multilingual education and its benefits for students.

One of the key advantages of technology integration in multilingual education is the ability to provide personalized and differentiated instruction. With the help of online platforms, students can access language learning materials tailored to their individual needs and proficiency levels. This allows them to progress at their own pace and receive immediate feedback, promoting a more student-centered approach to learning.

Moreover, technology offers a wide range of interactive tools and resources that can make language learning more engaging and enjoyable. For example, language learning apps and software provide opportunities for students to practice their language skills through interactive games, quizzes, and virtual conversations. These tools not only foster language acquisition but also promote cultural understanding and appreciation.

Another aspect of technology integration in multilingual education is the facilitation of communication and collaboration among students from different language backgrounds. Online platforms and video conferencing tools enable students to interact with peers from around the world, engaging in real-life conversations and cultural exchanges. This not only enhances language proficiency but also promotes global citizenship and intercultural competence.

Furthermore, technology can support teachers in designing and delivering effective multilingual curriculum. Online resources and digital textbooks provide access to a wide range of authentic materials, such as literature, videos, and podcasts, which can be incorporated into lesson plans. Additionally, technology allows for the creation and sharing of multimedia content, enabling teachers to design engaging and interactive language learning activities.

In conclusion, technology integration in multilingual education holds immense potential for students, offering personalized instruction, interactive tools, global communication opportunities, and enhanced curriculum design. As students interested in curriculum development and instructional design, exploring the possibilities of technology integration in multilingual education will equip you with the knowledge and skills necessary to create innovative and effective multilingual programs that cater to the diverse needs of learners in our interconnected world.

Chapter 5: Assessing Multilingual Students

Formative Assessment Strategies

In the world of education, assessment plays a crucial role in gauging students' understanding and progress. However, traditional assessment methods often fall short in truly capturing students' learning and providing valuable feedback for improvement. This is where formative assessment strategies come into play. Formative assessment is not just about testing students' knowledge; it is a dynamic process that helps students actively engage in their own learning journey. In this subchapter, we will explore various formative assessment strategies that can enhance your learning experience and empower you to take ownership of your education.

One effective formative assessment strategy is self-assessment. By evaluating your own work, you can identify your strengths and weaknesses, set goals, and track your progress. This can be done through reflection journals, self-evaluation rubrics, or peer feedback sessions. Self-assessment not only fosters metacognitive skills but also builds self-confidence and motivation.

Another powerful formative assessment strategy is the use of questioning techniques. Asking thought-provoking questions not only stimulates critical thinking but also allows teachers to gauge students' understanding. Teachers can employ techniques such as think-pair-share, where students discuss their ideas with a partner before sharing with the whole class. This strategy encourages active participation and provides an opportunity for students to learn from each other.

Peer assessment is another valuable formative assessment strategy. Collaborating with your peers to provide constructive feedback on each other's work not only strengthens your understanding of the subject matter but also enhances your communication and teamwork skills. This can be done through peer editing, group discussions, or student-led presentations. Peer assessment promotes a supportive learning environment and encourages students to take responsibility for their own learning.

Incorporating technology into formative assessment is becoming increasingly popular. Online quizzes, interactive games, and digital portfolios allow for immediate feedback and personalized learning experiences. Technology also enables teachers to track students' progress more efficiently and provide targeted interventions when necessary.

In conclusion, formative assessment strategies are powerful tools that can transform your learning experience. By actively engaging in self-assessment, utilizing effective questioning techniques, embracing peer assessment, and leveraging technology, you can take control of your education and maximize your learning potential. Remember, assessment is not just about grades; it is about empowering yourself to become a lifelong learner.

Summative Assessment Strategies

In the realm of education, assessments play a crucial role in evaluating student learning and measuring the effectiveness of instruction. Summative assessments, in particular, are designed to assess students' understanding and knowledge acquisition at the end of a learning unit or course. These assessments provide valuable insights into students' overall performance, helping educators identify areas of improvement and make informed decisions about curriculum development and instructional design.

This subchapter explores various summative assessment strategies that students can employ to showcase their learning and demonstrate their mastery of a subject. By understanding these strategies, students will be better equipped to excel in their assessments and showcase their full potential.

One effective summative assessment strategy is the traditional written exam. These exams require students to answer questions based on their knowledge and understanding of the course material. To excel in written exams, students should engage in regular revision, create comprehensive study guides, and practice past exam papers. It is important to manage time effectively during exams, allocate sufficient time for each question, and ensure clear and concise answers.

Another valuable summative assessment strategy is the creation of portfolios. Portfolios allow students to showcase their work and demonstrate their learning progress throughout a course. Students can include various artifacts such as essays, projects, presentations, and reflections. By curating their best work, students can provide evidence of their skills, knowledge, and growth over time.

Group projects also serve as effective summative assessments. These projects encourage collaboration, problem-solving, and critical thinking skills. Students must work together to complete a project that demonstrates their understanding of the subject matter. When participating in group projects, students should effectively communicate, contribute their unique perspectives, and divide tasks equitably.

In addition to these strategies, oral presentations, performances, and practical assessments are also common summative assessment methods. These assessment strategies allow students to showcase their understanding in a more interactive and practical manner. By engaging in these activities, students can demonstrate their ability to apply knowledge and skills in real-world contexts.

In conclusion, summative assessment strategies are essential in evaluating student learning and informing curriculum development and instructional design. By familiarizing themselves with various strategies such as written exams, portfolios, group projects, oral presentations, performances, and practical assessments, students can actively demonstrate their knowledge, skills, and growth. Employing these strategies will not only enhance their academic performance but also equip them with essential skills for the future.

Authentic Assessment in Multilingual Education

In the realm of multilingual education, it is essential to develop effective assessment strategies that accurately reflect students' language proficiency and overall learning progress. Traditional assessment methods often fall short in capturing the complexity and diversity of language skills, particularly in multilingual contexts. This is where authentic assessment comes into play.

Authentic assessment in multilingual education refers to the evaluation of students' language abilities in real-life, meaningful contexts. It goes beyond the conventional paper-and-pencil tests and emphasizes the application of language skills in practical situations. Through authentic assessment, students are given opportunities to demonstrate their linguistic competencies in various communicative tasks, such as presentations, debates, or role-plays.

One of the primary goals of authentic assessment is to assess students' ability to use language effectively and meaningfully. By engaging students in authentic tasks, educators can observe how well students apply their language skills to solve real-world problems and communicate their ideas. This type of assessment not only measures language proficiency but also fosters critical thinking, creativity, and problem-solving skills.

Authentic assessment also acknowledges the diversity of languages and cultures in multilingual education. It recognizes the value of students' linguistic and cultural backgrounds and encourages them to utilize their linguistic repertoires to express themselves authentically. This approach promotes a more inclusive and culturally responsive learning environment, where students feel empowered to use their languages as a valuable asset.

In order to implement authentic assessment effectively, curriculum development and instructional design play crucial roles. Educators need to design tasks that align with the learning objectives and incorporate real-life situations that students are likely to encounter outside the classroom. They should also provide clear criteria for evaluation and offer constructive feedback to guide students' language development.

In conclusion, authentic assessment in multilingual education offers a more comprehensive and accurate evaluation of students' language abilities. It emphasizes the application of language skills in meaningful contexts, promotes critical thinking, and values students' linguistic and cultural backgrounds. Curriculum developers and instructional designers play a vital role in creating authentic assessment tasks that reflect the goals of multilingual education and empower students to use their languages effectively. By embracing authentic assessment, students can develop the necessary language skills to thrive in a multilingual and interconnected world.

Chapter 6: Creating Inclusive Multilingual Learning Environments

Culturally Responsive Teaching

Culturally Responsive Teaching: Embracing Diversity in the Classroom

In today's multicultural world, it is crucial for educators to adopt culturally responsive teaching practices to create inclusive learning environments for all students. Culturally Responsive Teaching (CRT) is an approach that recognizes and values the diverse cultural backgrounds of students, and uses this knowledge to design and implement effective instruction. This subchapter will provide an introduction to CRT and how it can be applied in curriculum development and instructional design.

Cultural diversity enriches the classroom experience, allowing students to learn from one another and develop a deeper understanding of different perspectives. However, without intentional efforts to address cultural differences, some students may feel marginalized or excluded. CRT aims to bridge this gap by ensuring that all students see themselves reflected in the curriculum and instructional methods.

One key aspect of CRT is the incorporation of culturally relevant content. By including materials, literature, and examples from various cultures, educators can make curriculum more relatable and engaging for students from different backgrounds. This approach not only enhances students' sense of belonging but also promotes critical thinking and encourages them to explore their own cultural identities.

Furthermore, instructional design in CRT focuses on incorporating diverse teaching strategies that accommodate different learning styles and cultural preferences. This approach recognizes that students have unique ways of understanding and processing information, and adapts instructional methods to meet their needs. For instance, collaborative learning activities and group discussions can foster a sense of community and encourage students to learn from one another's cultural experiences.

In addition to content and instructional strategies, CRT also emphasizes the importance of building positive relationships between teachers and students. By creating a respectful and inclusive classroom environment, educators can establish trust and open communication with their students. This enables students to feel comfortable expressing their ideas and concerns, leading to a deeper engagement in the learning process.

Overall, culturally responsive teaching is a powerful tool that promotes equity, diversity, and inclusivity in the classroom. By acknowledging and embracing the cultural backgrounds of students, educators can create a learning environment that celebrates diversity and empowers all learners. Through the integration of culturally relevant content, diverse instructional strategies, and positive teacher-student relationships, CRT helps students develop a strong sense of identity, fosters their academic success, and prepares them for an increasingly multicultural world.

As students pursuing curriculum development and instructional design, understanding and implementing culturally responsive teaching practices will be essential in creating inclusive and effective educational experiences. By embracing diversity and valuing cultural differences, you will be equipped to design curriculum and instructional methods that meet the needs of all learners, regardless of their cultural backgrounds.

Collaboration and Cooperation in Multilingual Classrooms

In today's globalized world, multilingual classrooms have become the norm rather than the exception. These classrooms bring together students from diverse linguistic and cultural backgrounds, creating a rich environment for learning and growth. However, they also present unique challenges that require collaboration and cooperation among students and educators.

Collaboration and cooperation are essential in multilingual classrooms to foster effective communication and understanding among students. When students work together, they have the opportunity to share their linguistic knowledge and cultural experiences, promoting a sense of inclusivity and mutual respect. Through collaboration, students can learn from one another and develop a deeper understanding of different languages and cultures.

One way to promote collaboration in multilingual classrooms is through group projects and activities. By assigning tasks that require students to work together, educators can encourage them to use their linguistic skills and cultural knowledge to solve problems and achieve common goals. This not only enhances their language proficiency but also helps them develop important teamwork and interpersonal skills that are essential in today's interconnected world.

Cooperation is equally important in multilingual classrooms. It involves students actively supporting and assisting one another in their language learning journey. For instance, more proficient speakers can help their peers who are still developing their language skills by providing guidance, feedback, and encouragement. This cooperative approach creates a supportive and inclusive classroom environment, where students feel comfortable taking risks and making mistakes, knowing that they have the support of their peers.

To facilitate collaboration and cooperation in multilingual classrooms, educators need to employ student-centered curriculum design. This approach places students at the center of the learning process and encourages their active engagement and participation. By incorporating activities that promote collaboration and cooperation, such as group discussions, peer teaching, and project-based learning, educators can create a dynamic and inclusive learning environment where students can thrive.

In conclusion, collaboration and cooperation are vital in multilingual classrooms. Through collaboration, students can learn from one another and develop a deeper understanding of different languages and cultures. Cooperation, on the other hand, promotes a supportive and inclusive classroom environment, where students actively support and assist one another in their language learning journey. By employing student-centered curriculum design and incorporating activities that foster collaboration and cooperation, educators can create a vibrant and enriching learning environment for their multilingual students.

Supporting Linguistic and Cultural Diversity

In today's increasingly interconnected world, linguistic and cultural diversity has become a defining characteristic of our societies. As students, it is essential to recognize the value and importance of embracing and supporting this diversity. This subchapter aims to shed light on the significance of linguistic and cultural diversity and provide insights on how to promote it through student-centered curriculum design.

Linguistic diversity refers to the variety of languages spoken by individuals within a particular community or society. It is a reflection of the rich tapestry of human culture and heritage. By recognizing and celebrating linguistic diversity, we can foster a sense of inclusivity and create an environment that respects and values different languages. This subchapter will explore strategies for incorporating multiple languages into the curriculum, such as bilingual or multilingual instruction, language exchange programs, and the use of resources in various languages.

Cultural diversity, on the other hand, encompasses the range of different cultural practices, beliefs, and traditions followed by individuals from diverse backgrounds. By promoting cultural diversity, we can encourage students to appreciate and respect different ways of life, fostering a sense of global citizenship. This subchapter will delve into the importance of integrating diverse cultural perspectives into the curriculum, including literature, art, history, and social studies, to provide students with a broader understanding of the world.

Moreover, this subchapter will emphasize the benefits of linguistic and cultural diversity in education. Research shows that exposure to different languages and cultures enhances cognitive development, critical thinking skills, and problem-solving abilities. It also promotes empathy, tolerance, and open-mindedness among students. By embracing linguistic and cultural diversity, students can gain a global perspective, develop intercultural competence, and become effective communicators in a multicultural world.

To support linguistic and cultural diversity effectively, this subchapter will provide practical suggestions for curriculum development and instructional design. It will highlight the importance of creating inclusive classrooms, fostering a positive learning environment, and incorporating student voices and experiences into the curriculum. The subchapter will also discuss the role of educators in promoting linguistic and cultural diversity, including professional development opportunities and ongoing support.

By embracing linguistic and cultural diversity, students can embark on a journey of self-discovery, broaden their horizons, and become active participants in shaping a more inclusive and equitable society. Through student-centered curriculum design, we can create educational experiences that celebrate diversity, empower learners, and promote a more harmonious and interconnected world.

Chapter 7: Implementing Multilingual Curriculum

Teacher Training and Professional Development

For students interested in the fields of curriculum development and instructional design, understanding the importance of teacher training and professional development is essential. In this subchapter, we will explore the significance of ongoing training and development for educators and how it contributes to the success of student-centered curriculum design.

Teacher training and professional development are integral aspects of creating effective educational systems. It is through these initiatives that educators are equipped with the necessary skills and knowledge to implement student-centered curriculum designs. By investing in continuous training, teachers can enhance their instructional practices, stay up-to-date with the latest pedagogical strategies, and meet the diverse needs of their students.

One of the key benefits of teacher training is the opportunity it provides for educators to develop a deep understanding of student-centered curriculum design. Through workshops, seminars, and collaborative learning experiences, teachers can explore innovative teaching methods that prioritize student engagement and active learning. They can learn how to create meaningful learning experiences that promote critical thinking, problem-solving, and creativity.

Moreover, professional development programs enable teachers to stay informed about advancements in technology and its integration into the classroom. In today's digital age, it is crucial for educators to be proficient in using educational technology tools to enhance instruction. Through training programs, teachers can familiarize themselves with various educational apps, online platforms, and digital resources that can enrich the learning experiences of their students.

Teacher training and professional development also provide a platform for educators to share their experiences and learn from one another. Collaborative learning environments allow teachers to exchange ideas, strategies, and best practices, fostering a community of educators who are committed to continuous improvement.

In conclusion, teacher training and professional development play a vital role in curriculum development and instructional design. By investing in ongoing training, educators can enhance their instructional practices, stay updated with the latest pedagogical strategies, and meet the diverse needs of their students. Through these initiatives, teachers can develop a deep understanding of student-centered curriculum design, incorporate technology into their instruction, and foster a collaborative learning community. As future curriculum developers and instructional designers, it is crucial for students to recognize the importance of teacher training and professional development in creating effective educational systems that prioritize student success.

Overcoming Barriers to Implementation

Implementing any new educational program or curriculum can be a challenging task. There are often various barriers that can hinder the successful execution of plans and ideas. In the realm of curriculum development and instructional design, it is crucial for students to understand these barriers and learn strategies to overcome them. This subchapter aims to shed light on the common barriers faced in implementing multilingual education programs and offers practical solutions to address them.

One of the main barriers to implementation is the resistance to change. Students need to recognize that change can be met with skepticism and resistance from various stakeholders, including teachers, parents, and administrators. However, it is important to communicate the benefits of multilingual education and emphasize the positive impact it can have on students' language proficiency, cognitive skills, and cultural awareness.

Another significant barrier is the lack of resources and funding. Multilingual education programs often require additional resources such as textbooks, teaching materials, and trained teachers. Students need to be aware of the importance of advocating for adequate funding and resources to ensure the successful implementation of these programs. They can explore creative solutions such as crowdfunding campaigns or partnerships with local organizations to secure the necessary resources.

Additionally, language policy and legislation can pose barriers to the implementation of multilingual education. Students should familiarize themselves with existing policies and laws related to language education in their respective contexts. They can engage in advocacy efforts to push for policy changes that support and promote multilingual education.

Moreover, cultural and societal attitudes towards multilingualism can act as barriers. Students need to understand that promoting multilingual education requires challenging the dominant monolingual mindset and embracing the value of linguistic diversity. They can organize awareness campaigns, cultural events, and language exchange programs to foster a positive attitude towards multilingualism within their communities.

Lastly, the lack of training and professional development for teachers can hinder the successful implementation of multilingual education programs. Students interested in curriculum development and instructional design should focus on designing comprehensive professional development programs for teachers, including workshops, seminars, and mentoring opportunities. By empowering teachers with the necessary skills and knowledge, the implementation process can become smoother and more effective.

In conclusion, overcoming barriers to implementation is crucial for the success of any educational program, especially in the context of multilingual education. By understanding and addressing common barriers such as resistance to change, lack of resources, language policy, cultural attitudes, and teacher training, students can play a significant role in ensuring the successful implementation of multilingual education programs. Through their dedication and advocacy efforts, they can contribute to creating inclusive and linguistically diverse educational environments for all students.

Monitoring and Evaluation of Multilingual Programs

In the realm of multilingual education, the successful implementation of programs hinges not only on effective curriculum design but also on continuous monitoring and evaluation. This subchapter aims to shed light on the significance of monitoring and evaluation in multilingual programs and provide students with insights into the key aspects of this crucial process.

Monitoring and evaluation play a vital role in ensuring the quality and effectiveness of multilingual programs. By systematically collecting and analyzing data, educators can gauge the progress and impact of these programs, identify areas that need improvement, and make informed decisions to enhance student learning outcomes.

One key aspect of monitoring and evaluation is the collection of data on student performance. This includes tracking students' language proficiency levels, academic achievements, and overall engagement in multilingual classrooms. By employing various assessment tools, such as standardized tests, portfolios, and observations, educators can gather valuable information about students' progress and identify any gaps in their learning.

Furthermore, monitoring and evaluation also involve assessing the effectiveness of instructional strategies and materials used in multilingual programs. This includes evaluating the appropriateness of teaching methods, curriculum materials, and resources in meeting the diverse needs of students. By soliciting feedback from students and conducting classroom observations, educators can gain insights into the strengths and weaknesses of their instructional practices and make necessary adjustments.

Another critical aspect of monitoring and evaluation is the evaluation of program outcomes and impact. This involves examining the long-term effects of multilingual education on students' language proficiency, academic achievement, and overall development. By analyzing data from standardized tests, surveys, and interviews, educators can determine the effectiveness of the program in achieving its goals and meeting the needs of students.

To ensure effective monitoring and evaluation, it is essential for educators to establish clear goals and objectives for their multilingual programs. This allows for a focused approach to data collection and analysis, enabling educators to measure progress accurately and make data-driven decisions.

In conclusion, monitoring and evaluation are integral components of multilingual programs. By systematically collecting and analyzing data on student performance, instructional strategies, and program outcomes, educators can ensure the quality and effectiveness of these programs. Through continuous monitoring and evaluation, educators can make informed decisions to enhance student learning outcomes and promote the success of multilingual education.

Chapter 8: Case Studies in Multilingual Education

Successful Multilingual Education Programs

In recent years, the importance of multilingual education has gained significant recognition worldwide. As students in an increasingly globalized society, it is crucial to understand the benefits and challenges of embracing multiple languages in our educational systems. This subchapter explores successful multilingual education programs that have been designed to address the needs of diverse student populations.

One exemplary multilingual education program is the Dual Language Immersion (DLI) model. DLI programs aim to foster bilingualism and biliteracy by providing instruction in two languages, typically one being the students' native language and the other a target language. Research has consistently shown that students in DLI programs outperform their monolingual peers in academic achievement, cognitive skills, and cultural awareness. Through carefully crafted curriculum and instructional design, DLI programs promote language proficiency, cross-cultural understanding, and academic excellence.

Another noteworthy program is Content and Language Integrated Learning (CLIL). CLIL programs integrate language learning with the study of academic subjects such as math, science, or social studies. This approach not only enhances students' language skills but also enables them to grasp complex concepts and develop critical thinking skills in a multilingual context. By immersing students in a language-rich environment, CLIL programs create authentic opportunities for language acquisition and content mastery.

Furthermore, the International Baccalaureate (IB) program offers an inclusive and rigorous multilingual curriculum that prepares students for success in a globalized world. The IB curriculum focuses on developing students' language skills, intercultural understanding, and knowledge of global issues. By encouraging students to explore different cultures and perspectives, the IB program fosters open-mindedness, empathy, and effective communication skills across languages.

Successful multilingual education programs share common characteristics. They prioritize student-centered curriculum design, which recognizes students' diverse linguistic backgrounds and adapts instructional strategies accordingly. These programs also emphasize the importance of qualified and trained teachers who are proficient in the target languages and possess cultural competence.

As students interested in curriculum development and instructional design, it is essential to study successful multilingual education programs. By understanding their principles and strategies, we can contribute to the creation of inclusive educational environments that celebrate linguistic diversity and equip students with the necessary skills to thrive in an interconnected world.

Challenges and Lessons Learned

In the journey towards multilingual education and student-centered curriculum design, there are bound to be challenges along the way. As students, you are the driving force behind the implementation of these innovative approaches in the field of curriculum development and instructional design. This subchapter aims to shed light on some of the common challenges faced in this process and the valuable lessons learned throughout.

One of the primary challenges encountered when incorporating multilingual education is the lack of resources and materials. Many educational institutions have traditionally focused on monolingual approaches, making it difficult to find appropriate materials that cater to diverse linguistic backgrounds. However, this challenge also presents an opportunity for students to get creative and collaborate in developing their own resources. By leveraging technology and utilizing the vast resources available online, students can create multilingual materials that reflect their own cultural and linguistic diversity.

Another challenge that arises in student-centered curriculum design is the resistance to change from both educators and students themselves. Some educators may be hesitant to adopt new approaches, fearing that it may disrupt the established teaching methods. Similarly, students may resist the shift towards a more student-centered approach, as they may be accustomed to a teacher-led learning environment. Overcoming this challenge requires effective communication and continuous dialogue between all stakeholders. By highlighting the benefits of student-centered curriculum design, such as increased engagement and personalized learning experiences, educators and students can be encouraged to embrace the change.

Furthermore, the implementation of student-centered curriculum design may also face challenges related to assessment and evaluation. Traditional assessment methods often focus on measuring rote memorization and standardized test scores, which may not accurately reflect the holistic development of students in a multilingual education setting. It is crucial for students to advocate for alternative assessment methods that align with the goals of student-centered curriculum design, such as project-based assessments, portfolios, and self-reflection exercises.

Throughout the process of exploring multilingual education and student-centered curriculum design, valuable lessons are learned. Students realize the importance of collaboration, adaptability, and open-mindedness. They learn to appreciate the unique strengths and perspectives that each individual brings to the learning environment. They understand the significance of embracing diversity and creating an inclusive space that celebrates different cultures and languages.

In conclusion, the challenges faced in implementing multilingual education and student-centered curriculum design are opportunities for growth and innovation. By addressing the lack of resources, overcoming resistance to change, and redefining assessment methods, students can lead the way towards a more inclusive and effective educational system. The lessons learned throughout this process will shape the future of curriculum development and instructional design, empowering students to create their own words and worlds.

Best Practices in Multilingual Education

In today's globalized world, the ability to communicate in multiple languages has become increasingly essential. Multilingual education plays a crucial role in promoting cross-cultural understanding, fostering linguistic diversity, and empowering individuals to thrive in a multicultural society. This subchapter, "Best Practices in Multilingual Education," aims to provide students with valuable insights into the principles and strategies that underpin effective curriculum development and instructional design in multilingual education.

1. Embrace student-centered approaches: Multilingual education should prioritize students' needs, interests, and learning styles. By incorporating student-centered approaches, educators can create an inclusive and engaging environment that encourages active participation and promotes deeper learning.

2. Promote language immersion: Immersion programs allow students to learn a second or third language in a natural, authentic context. Creating opportunities for students to use the target language in real-life situations fosters language acquisition and fluency.

3. Develop culturally relevant materials: Multilingual education should celebrate and integrate students' cultural backgrounds. By incorporating culturally relevant materials, educators can enhance students' sense of identity and pride, while also promoting intercultural understanding.

4. Implement a balanced bilingual approach: A balanced bilingual approach ensures that both the first language (L1) and the second language (L2) are valued and developed. This approach recognizes the

cognitive, linguistic, and academic benefits of maintaining strong skills in the L1 while acquiring proficiency in the L2.

5. Foster collaboration and peer interaction: Collaborative learning experiences enable students to learn from and with their peers. Group activities, discussions, and project-based learning encourage language practice and the development of communication skills.

6. Utilize technology as a tool: Integrating technology into multilingual education can enhance language acquisition and provide opportunities for independent learning. Online resources, language-learning apps, and virtual exchange programs can supplement classroom instruction and expand students' exposure to different languages and cultures.

7. Provide ongoing support: Multilingual education requires ongoing support for students, educators, and families. Providing professional development opportunities, access to language resources, and fostering partnerships with families can contribute to the success of multilingual education programs.

By incorporating these best practices into curriculum development and instructional design, students can benefit from an enriching and effective multilingual education experience. This subchapter equips students with the knowledge and tools to empower themselves and others as they navigate the interconnected world of multilingualism.

Chapter 9: Advocacy for Multilingual Education

Promoting Multilingualism in Education Policies

In today's increasingly interconnected world, multilingualism has become a valuable asset for individuals and societies alike. Recognizing the importance of language diversity and its benefits, education policies worldwide are shifting towards promoting multilingualism in the classroom. This subchapter delves into the significance of including multilingualism in education policies, with a particular focus on curriculum development and instructional design.

Multilingual education is a student-centered approach that recognizes and values the linguistic resources students bring to the classroom. It encourages the use and development of multiple languages, fostering a sense of inclusivity and creating a more enriching learning environment. By incorporating students' first languages and providing opportunities for them to learn additional languages, education policies can empower students to become competent, confident, and culturally aware global citizens.

Curriculum development plays a crucial role in promoting multilingualism in education policies. It involves designing a curriculum that reflects the linguistic diversity of the student population and ensures equal access to quality education for all. This includes providing language support programs, bilingual education models, and resources that cater to the needs of multilingual learners. By adopting a student-centered curriculum design, education policies can create an inclusive and engaging learning experience that embraces students' linguistic backgrounds.

Instructional design goes hand in hand with curriculum development in promoting multilingualism. It involves the creation of effective teaching strategies and materials that cater to the diverse linguistic needs of students. Instructional designers play a vital role in developing pedagogical approaches that facilitate language acquisition, provide language support, and promote bilingualism. By incorporating innovative teaching methods, technology, and culturally relevant materials, instructional designers can enhance the learning experience and help students develop proficiency in multiple languages.

Promoting multilingualism in education policies is not only about language acquisition but also about fostering intercultural competence and understanding. By exposing students to different languages and cultures, education policies can foster respect, empathy, and appreciation for diversity. This prepares students to navigate the globalized world, develop intercultural communication skills, and bridge cultural gaps.

In conclusion, promoting multilingualism in education policies is essential for preparing students for the challenges and opportunities of the 21st century. Curriculum development and instructional design play a crucial role in implementing these policies, ensuring that students receive an inclusive, culturally rich, and linguistically diverse education. By embracing multilingualism, education policies can empower students to become global citizens who contribute positively to their communities and the world at large.

Engaging Communities and Parents

In the journey towards student-centered curriculum design, one of the most crucial aspects is the involvement of communities and parents. By actively engaging these stakeholders, educators can create a rich and supportive learning environment that nurtures the growth and development of students.

Communities play a vital role in education, as they provide a broader perspective and understanding of the world outside the classroom. By collaborating with community members, educators can integrate real-world experiences into the curriculum, making learning more relevant and meaningful for students. This can be achieved through guest speakers, field trips, and community service projects, where students can apply their knowledge and skills in real-life situations. These interactions also expose students to different cultural perspectives and foster a sense of empathy and understanding, preparing them to become global citizens.

Parents are equally important partners in the educational journey. They possess valuable insights into their child's strengths, weaknesses, and interests. By actively involving parents in curriculum development, educators can tailor the learning experience to the individual needs of each student. This can be achieved through regular communication, parent-teacher conferences, and workshops that provide parents with the necessary tools to support their child's learning at home. When parents are engaged, they become an integral part of the educational process, reinforcing the skills and knowledge acquired at school and creating a seamless learning experience for students.

In addition to their role in curriculum development, communities and parents can also contribute to the assessment and evaluation of student learning. By involving them in the design of assessment tools and rubrics, educators can ensure that the evaluation process is comprehensive and fair. This collaborative approach to assessment fosters transparency and accountability, as parents and community members have a clear understanding of the learning goals and expectations.

Overall, engaging communities and parents in the curriculum development and instructional design process enhances the quality of education and promotes student success. By harnessing the collective wisdom and experiences of these stakeholders, educators can create a dynamic and inclusive learning environment that prepares students for the challenges of the 21st century.

Empowering Students as Language Advocates

In the field of education, there has been a growing recognition of the importance of multilingualism and the benefits it brings to individuals and communities. As our world becomes more interconnected, the ability to communicate in multiple languages has become a valuable skill. It not only opens doors to diverse cultures and perspectives but also enhances cognitive abilities and problem-solving skills. In this subchapter, we will discuss the concept of empowering students as language advocates and how this can be achieved through student-centered curriculum design.

Language advocacy refers to the active promotion and support of multilingualism and the recognition of the value of all languages. As students, you have the power to become advocates for language diversity in your schools and communities. By embracing and celebrating diverse languages, you can contribute to creating an inclusive and supportive environment for all learners.

To empower students as language advocates, curriculum development and instructional design play a crucial role. Student-centered curriculum design focuses on the needs, interests, and strengths of individual learners. It encourages active participation, critical thinking, and collaboration. By incorporating multilingualism and language advocacy into the curriculum, you can develop a sense of ownership and responsibility among students.

One way to empower students as language advocates is by creating opportunities for them to use and showcase their linguistic skills. This can be done through language clubs, cultural events, or language exchange programs. By actively engaging in these activities, students not only strengthen their language proficiency but also develop a sense of pride and identity in their linguistic heritage.

Another strategy is to integrate language advocacy into various subject areas. For example, in social studies, students can explore the contributions of different cultures and languages to society. In science, they can investigate the impact of language on communication and understanding. By connecting language advocacy to different disciplines, students can see the relevance and importance of multilingualism in various aspects of their lives.

In conclusion, empowering students as language advocates is essential in promoting multilingualism and fostering inclusive learning environments. Through student-centered curriculum design, students can actively participate in language advocacy and develop a sense of ownership and pride in their linguistic skills. By integrating language advocacy into various subject areas, students can see the relevance and value of multilingualism in different contexts. As students, you have the power to make a difference in promoting language diversity and creating a more inclusive society.

Chapter 10: Future Directions in Multilingual Education

Innovations in Multilingual Curriculum Design

As students, we are living in a rapidly globalizing world, where multilingualism has become the norm rather than the exception. The ability to communicate and navigate multiple languages is a valuable skill that opens doors to new opportunities and experiences. In recognition of this, curriculum developers and instructional designers have been actively working to create innovative approaches to multilingual education. This subchapter titled "Innovations in Multilingual Curriculum Design" explores some of the groundbreaking advancements in this field that are shaping our educational experiences.

One of the key innovations in multilingual curriculum design is the shift towards a student-centered approach. Gone are the days when language learning was confined to textbooks and grammar exercises. Instead, curriculum developers are now focusing on creating authentic and meaningful learning experiences that reflect students' personal interests and cultural backgrounds. This approach not only enhances students' motivation and engagement but also allows them to develop a deeper understanding and appreciation for different languages and cultures.

Another significant innovation in multilingual curriculum design is the integration of technology. With the advent of digital tools and resources, students now have access to a wealth of language learning opportunities. From online language courses to language exchange platforms, technology has made it easier than ever for students to practice and develop their language skills. Furthermore, the use of virtual reality and augmented reality in language learning has opened up new possibilities for immersive and interactive learning experiences.

In addition to these advancements, multilingual curriculum designers are also exploring the concept of translanguaging. Traditionally, languages have been taught separately, with little emphasis on their interconnectedness. However, translanguaging recognizes that multilingual individuals naturally draw on all their linguistic resources to communicate and make meaning. By embracing translanguaging in curriculum design, students are encouraged to use all their languages in the learning process, fostering a deeper understanding and appreciation for linguistic diversity.

Overall, innovations in multilingual curriculum design are transforming the way we learn languages. By adopting student-centered approaches, integrating technology, and embracing translanguaging, curriculum developers and instructional designers are creating a more inclusive and effective learning environment for all students. As students, it is important for us to be aware of these innovations and actively engage with them to make the most of our multilingual education.

Incorporating Global Perspectives

In today's interconnected world, it is essential for students to develop a global perspective in their education. As the world becomes increasingly interconnected, understanding different cultures, languages, and perspectives is crucial for success in the 21st century. This subchapter explores the importance of incorporating global perspectives into curriculum development and instructional design, and provides practical strategies for students interested in curriculum development and instructional design.

A global perspective allows students to understand and appreciate the diversity of our world. By learning about different cultures, languages, and perspectives, students can develop a broader understanding of global issues and become more empathetic towards others. This understanding can lead to the development of essential skills such as critical thinking, problem-solving, and effective communication.

Incorporating global perspectives into curriculum development involves intentionally designing learning experiences that expose students to diverse perspectives. This can be done through the inclusion of literature, videos, guest speakers, and virtual exchanges that showcase different cultures and perspectives. By incorporating these elements, students can develop a more comprehensive understanding of global issues and learn to think critically about them.

Instructional design plays a crucial role in incorporating global perspectives into the classroom. It involves creating engaging and interactive learning experiences that expose students to a variety of global perspectives. This can be achieved through project-based learning, collaborative activities, and discussions that encourage students to explore different cultures and perspectives. By designing instruction that is culturally responsive and inclusive, students can develop a deeper understanding of global issues and develop essential skills for success in a globalized world.

For students interested in curriculum development and instructional design, it is important to stay informed about current global issues and trends. This can be done through reading books, attending conferences, and participating in professional development opportunities. Additionally, networking with professionals in the field can provide valuable insights and opportunities for collaboration.

In conclusion, incorporating global perspectives into curriculum development and instructional design is essential for students in today's interconnected world. By understanding and appreciating different cultures and perspectives, students can develop essential skills and become more empathetic towards others. Through intentional curriculum design and instructional strategies, students can develop a global perspective that will prepare them for success in the 21st century.

Research and Trends in Multilingual Education

Introduction:

In recent years, there has been a growing interest in multilingual education as educators and policymakers recognize the importance of preparing students for an increasingly interconnected world. This subchapter aims to explore the latest research and trends in multilingual education, providing insights that can help students in the fields of curriculum development and instructional design understand the evolving landscape.

1.   The   Benefits   of   Multilingual   Education: Research has consistently shown that multilingual education offers numerous cognitive, social, and cultural benefits to students. Multilingual individuals have enhanced problem-solving skills, improved memory, and greater mental flexibility. They also develop a deeper understanding and appreciation for different cultures, fostering empathy and global citizenship.

2.   Language   Acquisition   Theories: Understanding the theories behind language acquisition is crucial for designing effective multilingual education programs. This subchapter outlines key theories such as the Critical Period Hypothesis, Input Hypothesis, and Sociocultural Theory, providing students with a foundation to develop curriculum designs that optimize language learning.

3.   Bilingualism   and   Biliteracy: The concept of bilingualism has evolved beyond mere language proficiency. The focus has shifted towards developing biliteracy skills, which involve not only speaking, listening, reading, and writing in

multiple languages but also understanding and critically analyzing texts in both languages. Students will explore innovative instructional strategies that promote biliteracy development.

4.   Technology   in   Multilingual   Education: Technology has revolutionized education, and multilingual education is no exception. This subchapter discusses the latest trends in using technology to enhance language learning, such as language learning apps, online collaborative platforms, and virtual reality. Students will gain insights into designing technology-integrated multilingual curriculum.

5.   Multilingual   Education   Policies: National and international policies play a crucial role in shaping multilingual education practices. This section explores current policies and initiatives promoting multilingualism, such as bilingual education programs, dual-language immersion, and content and language integrated learning (CLIL). Students will examine the impact of these policies on curriculum design and instructional practices.

Conclusion:

As the world becomes increasingly interconnected, multilingual education is gaining prominence. By staying updated with the latest research and trends in this field, students specializing in curriculum development and instructional design can create effective and inclusive educational experiences for multilingual learners. From understanding the benefits of multilingualism to exploring innovative instructional strategies and technology integration, this subchapter equips students with the knowledge and tools necessary to design student-centered multilingual education programs that foster language proficiency, cultural awareness, and global citizenship.

Conclusion: Reflecting on Multilingual Education Journey

As we come to the end of this book, it is essential for students engaged in curriculum development and instructional design to reflect on their multilingual education journey. Throughout this journey, we have explored the intricacies of multilingual education and how it can be effectively incorporated into student-centered curriculum design.

In our exploration, we have emphasized the importance of embracing linguistic diversity and recognizing the unique strengths that multilingual students bring to the classroom. We have delved into the various models of multilingual education, such as dual language programs, bilingual education, and immersion programs, understanding their benefits and challenges.

One of the key takeaways from our discussion is the need for a student-centered approach to curriculum design. By placing students at the center of their own learning, we empower them to take ownership of their education and celebrate their linguistic and cultural backgrounds. This approach ensures that multilingual students are not only included but also thrive in the educational setting.

Throughout this book, we have also highlighted the significance of creating inclusive learning environments that foster cultural understanding and promote the value of multilingualism. By incorporating culturally relevant materials, encouraging peer collaboration, and providing opportunities for students to share their languages and cultures, we can create a truly inclusive and enriching educational experience for all.

As curriculum developers and instructional designers, it is also crucial for us to continuously reflect on our practices and adapt them to the ever-evolving needs of multilingual learners. This means staying informed about current research, engaging in professional development, and seeking feedback from students and colleagues. By doing so, we can ensure that our curriculum designs are relevant, effective, and responsive to the diverse needs of our students.

In conclusion, the journey of multilingual education is an ongoing process that requires dedication, open-mindedness, and a commitment to inclusivity. By embracing linguistic diversity, adopting a student-centered approach, and creating inclusive learning environments, we can unlock the full potential of multilingual learners. Let us continue to explore, innovate, and advocate for multilingual education, ensuring that all students have the opportunity to thrive and succeed in a globalized world.